A MUSIC NERD'S TRIVIA JAM

BOB CUTLER

Press Roll Press

Press Roll Press

The purpose of this book is to entertain and educate.
It is a collection of non-fiction music trivia covering popular music, songs, artists, lyrics, band members, record labels and music industry information available from a variety of public sources.

Copyright © 2021 by Robert F. Cutler

All rights reserved, including the right to reproduce this book
or portions thereof in any form whatsoever.

Book Design & Layout: Kathi Castelluccio
Cover Art & Illustrations: Jenna Castelluccio

The author is available for public discussions, radio or podcast segments, and special events in the context of music history, trivia and lively pop music dialog..

Contact: bcutler@sbcglobal.net

Printed in the United States of America

ISBN: 978-1-7369020-1-1

Some Choice Comments & Faint Praise

> *Why do you always have to drum your fingers on the kitchen table?*
> — Bob's mom

> *Hey, you tore a hole in my Naugahyde chair with those old sticks!*
> — Bob's dad

> *Why can't you guys play a little quieter?* — Bob's uncle Al

> *I used to like that song, but your analysis has kinda ruined it for me...*
> — Several dates gone bad

> *What are you going to do with music? How are you going to make a decent living?*
> — Bob's impatient, former college girlfriend

> *I really like this song, but please stop drumming on the dashboard!*
> — Another ex-girlfriend

> *He's a little obsessed with this stuff...* — Several of Bob's friends and family members

> *I can't believe you correctly guessed Bobbie Gentry!*
> — Bob after losing a 30-dinner bet to his wife, Michele, after the song "Ode To Billie Joe" was playing on the car radio

> *Go run around the cul-de-sac a few times!*
> — Bob to his kids when they were young and had way too much energy

> *Who do you think you are, Mr. Big Stuff?* — Singer, Jean Knight

Publishers tend to put praise and reviewers' comments at the very front of books to help sway the buyer. These little asides and quotes won't likely affect your decision to dive into this book, but here's a slightly different and offbeat version just for the record.

Dedication

To my wonderful wife, Michele, who has abided decades of my music obsession, chatter and commentary. She continues to listen to me and express interest in what lights me up. She is an incredible person, and she really loves music, too. Michele, you are an amazing life partner, and the true love of my life!

And to our circle of good friends and family, including a close-knit group known as, Tour de Friends. We have collectively shared many years of laughter and music discussion during weekend get-togethers, dinners, family gatherings and marathon trivia games.

And a very special thanks to the amazing friend and designer, Kathi Castelluccio, and her talented, artistic daughter, Jenna. You both really, really helped to bring this project to life!

I want you all to know how much I value our friendships, mutual love of music, and our camaraderie. And just like music, you are truly life-affirming!

Bob Cutler, 2021

(Looking) Forward – Playing the Intro

I'm guessing you are a music fan, too, or you probably wouldn't have picked up this trivia book. Thanks in advance for taking a look and trying your hand at the questions in this jam session.

I wrote this book during the COVID-19 pandemic. After retiring from a real job, I had a lot more time to put these questions together from scratch. The categories and content here have been bouncing around in my head for quite some time. As with most things like this, it truly took on a life of its own, resulting in several hundred questions for music nerds like me.

I approached this book by lobbing questions at you from a variety of musical genres and decades. And don't worry, I won't leave you hanging. I have included the answers for each category at the end of the book.

This quiz book is really about an accumulated catalog of pop and rock knowledge, background info, trivia bits and interesting facts. A smattering of bands, songwriters, and even some pop music lyrics, are represented. And there are some questions on jazz, blues, rap, movie and sports music, and even a light touch of classical. For die-hard fans, there are questions on rock band personnel, record labels, and albums in an effort to make this book a bit more diverse. Hopefully you will find some of this stuff challenging and educational, and that you're able to pick up a few interesting musical nuggets along the way.

BTW – there is no scoring system here. After going through these questions, you'll know what you know. And perhaps you'll know what you didn't know before. So please enjoy this music trivia jam session, and don't get discouraged if you feel a little overwhelmed at times. It's all good!

And finally, as Ringo Starr says quite frequently, "Peace and love!"

Play List

▲ A MUSIC NERD'S TRIVIA JAM

Session 1: Band Names & Personnel	1
Session 2: Cover Versions & Originals	7
Session 3: Performers & Pioneers	11
Session 4: The Beatles	15
Session 5: Drummers	17
Session 6: Songwriters	19
Session 7: Song Titles & Lyrics	25
Session 8: Record Albums	29
Session 9: Flip Sides	33
Session 10: Supergroups & Collaborations	35
Session 11: Record Labels	37
Session 12: Radio, TV & Movies	39
Session 13: Music Venues & Festivals	43
Session 14: Sports + Music = Fun	45
Session 15: Classical	47
Session 16: Jazz & Blues	49
Session 17: Rap & Hip Hop	51
Session 18: Musical Instruments	53
Session 19: The 1960s	55
Session 20: The 1970s	57
Session 21: The 1980s & Beyond	59
Session 22: Copycats	61
Trivia Jam Answers	63

Session 1: Band Names & Personnel

Session 1: Band Names & Personnel

1. Members of Led Zeppelin briefly toured in 1968 under a different band name before becoming Led Zeppelin. What was the pre-Zeppelin band name?

2. Bob Dylan's backing band became known as The Band when they began making their own records. What band name did they use before joining Dylan?

3. Which member of The Zombies formed a new band using his last name in 1970? Name the Top 20 hit record released under this new band name.

4. Loggins & Messina were a successful '70s pop/rock duo with hit songs like "Your Mama Don't Dance." Name the country-rock band that Jim Messina was a member of before joining up with Kenny Loggins.

5. Canadian rock group The Guess Who disbanded in the early '70s after a successful string of hit records. Several members

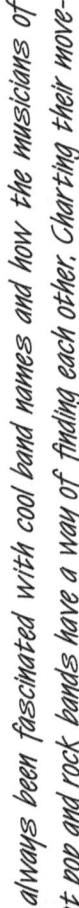

I've always been fascinated with cool band names and how the musicians of great pop and rock bands have a way of finding each other. Charting their movement from one band to another is like mapping musical genealogy.

of the band reformed under what name? And name one of their biggest hits.

6. After the '60s band The Turtles disbanded, two founding members and frontmen Mark Volman and Howard Kaylan formed a new band under what name?

7. Who was the female lead singer of Jefferson Airplane, and later Jefferson Starship, and then Starship? Name the band that she was in before joining Jefferson Airplane.

8. What was the name of the '60s pop group that Kenny Rogers led before becoming a successful solo artist? And name their first big hit song from 1968.

9. "Mississippi Queen" was a hit record for which American band in 1970?

10. Although not as well known, NRBQ has been a recording and performing rock band for several decades. What do the band's initials NRBQ stand for?

11. What is the origin of the band name the Bee Gees?

12. The amazingly talented musician, singer, and songwriter Todd Rundgren was in two bands from the late '60s to the early '70s before launching his successful solo career. Name both of those bands.

13. What is the common word found in the names of the two '70s bands that had the hit songs "One Fine Morning" and "Love Grows (Where My Rosemary Goes)"?

14. Name a band or solo artist in any musical genre that has a U.S. state in its name.

Session 1: Band Names & Personnel

15. Which long-running and well-known rock trio became commonly known as "That Little Ol' Band From Texas"?

16. Jimmie Vaughan, brother of the late great Stevie Ray Vaughan, was the lead guitarist in which popular Texas blues-rock band formed in the mid-'70s?

17. The late Gerry Rafferty, who had a Top 10 record with the song "Baker Street" in the late '70s, was previously in which band, and what was their hit record from 1973?

18. Curtis Mayfield was in which '60s Chicago soul group before his solo career produced hits like "Superfly" and "Freddie's Dead"? And which other great Chicago soul singer was in the same group before he also went solo?

19. Name the rock band that guitarist/singer Joe Walsh led in the early '70s before he went solo and eventually became a member of The Eagles.

20. Brothers Tim and Neil Finn were in various bands, including Crowded House, and they later teamed up as the Finn Brothers. What country are they from, and what was their band name on the 1980 hit song "I Got You"?

21. After Eric Burdon departed as the lead singer of the popular '60s band The Animals, he recorded the hit song "Spill the Wine" in 1970 with which American group?

22. On their first album, the band Chicago was initially named The Chicago Transit Authority. Name the Chicago university where several of the original band members met.

23. Name the two brothers and founding members of The Kinks.

24. Name the original members of The Grateful Dead.

25. Name Elvis Presley's drummer and his guitar player, who both played on many of his records and performed with him in concert.

26. Name a rock group that has, or had, blood brothers in the band.

27. Name the two founding members/musicians/songwriters of Steely Dan. And what is the origin of their band name?

28. What is the connection between the early '70s folk/pop music duo, Seals & Crofts, and the mid-'70s folk/pop duo, England Dan & John Ford Coley?

29. Name the famous pop music parents of the members of the '90s trio Wilson Phillips.

30. Which female singing group actually sang on the hit record "He's a Rebel" instead of The Crystals, credited on the record label?

31. As of 2021, how many of the original members of the Bee Gees are "stayin' alive"?

32. After the band Uncle Tupelo broke up in the '90s, two of the original band members went their separate ways & formed which two successful bands?

33. Skunk Baxter played lead guitar and some inspired solos on several Steely Dan songs. Skunk was a member of which other best-selling, well-known band from the '70s and beyond?

34. The late singer, songwriter, and producer Sylvia Robinson, known as Sylvia on her sultry 1973 hit "Pillow Talk," was in which singing duo from the '50s?

Session 1: Band Names & Personnel

35. Which groundbreaking British band from the late '60s, early '70s was singer/songwriter and guitarist Dave Mason a member of when he wrote the well-known and popular song "Feelin' Alright"?

36. Ray Charles is one of the most important and influential artists of the modern era. For many years, he recorded and toured with a group of female backing singers. What were they called?

37. Name any current or past member of Ringo Starr's All-Starr Band.

Session 2: Cover Versions & Originals

38. Which early Motown song was covered by both The Beatles and The Rolling Stones? And name the original singer.

39. Name the original artists who recorded the following songs that were covered by The Beatles.
    a) "Act Naturally"
    b) "Boys"
    c) "Roll Over Beethoven"
    d) "Dizzy, Miss Lizzy"
    e) "Twist and Shout"
    f) "Please Mr. Postman"

40. Who wrote and recorded the original version of "Black Magic Woman" before it was a Top 10 hit for Santana in the early '70s?

41. The first hit record in the early '70s for Creedence Clear-

Being a music nerd, I really enjoy hearing different interpretations of the same songs, and comparing covers to originals. Talented artists can often make cover versions more popular than the originals. Early on, I often didn't realize how many of my favorite songs were actually great covers.

water Revival was a cover of the song "Susie Q." Name the singer who recorded the original version.

42. Which band had a hit record in the early '70s with their cover of the car song "Hot Rod Lincoln"?

43. In the late '90s, rock band Pearl Jam covered an old pop song from the early '60s, "Last Kiss." Name the artist who had the original hit with this song.

44. Which Bruce Springsteen song was a hit record for The Pointer Sisters in the late '70s?

45. "All the Young Dudes" was a big '70s hit song for Mott the Hoople. Which pop music icon wrote this song and recorded his own version?

46. Name the '80s female group from the U.K. that had a hit with their cover of the song "Venus," originally by Shocking Blue.

47. Which well-known singer/songwriter and music icon wrote "Blinded by the Light," which became a No. 1 hit record for Manfred Mann's Earth Band in the early '70s?

48. "I Hear You Knocking" was a hit record for Dave Edmunds in the early '70s. The song was originally a hit record in 1955 by which New Orleans R&B singer?

49. Which contemporary rock group recorded a cover of the early '80s song "Africa" in 2018, making it a hit again, thirty-six years after the original by Toto?

Session 2: Cover Versions & Originals

50. Rick Derringer, founding member and lead singer of the '60s band The McCoys ("Hang On Sloopy"), went on to write and record a Top 40 hit record in the early '70s, "Rock and Roll, Hoochie Koo." Who recorded the first version of this song before Rick Derringer released his own version two years later?

51. The Raiders, formerly Paul Revere & the Raiders, had a No. 1 hit with a cover of "Indian Reservation" in 1971. Who recorded this song several years earlier but with less chart-topping success than The Raiders' version?

52. In the '70s, Ringo Starr had a big hit with a cover version of "You're Sixteen." Which rockabilly singer had the original hit with this song back in the early '60s?

53. Name the Beatles song that was given to The Rolling Stones to record in the Stones' early years, before The Beatles had their own hit version of the song.

54. Who recorded the original version of the song "Hound Dog," which was an early hit record for Elvis Presley?

55. Name the artist who had the highest-charting version of the hit song "I Heard It Through the Grapevine."

56. Who had the original 1967 hit with the song "You've Made Me So Very Happy" that became a huge hit for Blood, Sweat & Tears two years later?

57. Who recorded the original version of the popular song "I Fought The Law"?

58. Who recorded the original version of the mid-'60s hit by The Animals "Don't Let Me Be Misunderstood"?

59. Jackie Wilson's '60s hit record "(Your Love Keeps Lifting Me) Higher and Higher" was remade a decade later at a much slower tempo by which popular '70s female singer?

60. In the early '60s, The Valentinos recorded the song "Lookin' for a Love." The better-known version of this song was a '70s cover by which popular rock band from Boston?

61. In 1986, the rock band R.E.M. recorded a cover version of the song "Superman." Name the original band.

62. The '60s song "Here Comes My Baby" was written by Cat Stevens, but it was a Top 20 hit for which British pop group?

Session 3: Performers & Pioneers

Every so often a musical pioneer jumps out of the covered wagon in uncharted territory and creates chaos and genius. Prince, Chuck Berry, Ray Charles, Elvis, Marvin Gaye, Sam Cooke, Stevie Wonder, and The Beatles are just a few examples of artists who broke new musical ground.

63. Before Simon & Garfunkel were stars under their last names, what did this duo call themselves when first starting out?

64. Name the four '50s/'60s era singers who made up "The Million Dollar Quartet."

65. Which original member of the band Chicago accidentally killed himself playing with a gun that he didn't know was loaded?

66. Name the three well-known and very talented guitarists who were all members of The Yardbirds at various times in the band's history.

67. On the hit record "Soul Man" by Sam & Dave, which guitarist is called out by Sam Moore about halfway through the song? And name two other well-known bands that this guitarist was a member of.

68. Before becoming a well-known singer/songwriter, Sheryl

Crow was a backing vocalist for which famous pop star?

69. Name the collective of studio musicians that played on hundreds of hit records for various groups and solo artists in the '60s and '70s.

70. On Donovan's song "Mellow Yellow," who can be heard in the background whooping it up in various parts of the song?

71. Which famous singer sang a duet with Bob Dylan on the album *Nashville Skyline*?

72. Name the lead singer of the band Jethro Tull and the primary instrument he became known for.

73. Name one of Prince's female singers, musicians, and collaborators who had a successful solo career in her own right.

74. Which very famous pop star's real name is Reginald Dwight?

75. Name the female backing vocalist on the Rolling Stones song "Gimme Shelter" who the Stones called during their recording session to lend her vocals to the track.

76. In 1970, a band known as Free had a hit song with "All Right Now." Who was Free's lead singer, and which other popular rock band did he front after Free disbanded?

77. The Hollies had a hit record in 1969 with the song "He Ain't Heavy, He's My Brother." Which singer/songwriter and pop music icon also recorded a version of this song released a year later?

Session 3: Performers & Pioneers

78. Chrissie Hynde, the lead singer of The Pretenders, had a relationship and a child with which lead singer/songwriter of another well-known rock band from the '60s and '70s?

79. Name James Taylor's brother, who is also a singer-songwriter and folk musician.

80. Which song was Linda Ronstadt's only No. 1 hit according to *Billboard's* Hot 100 song chart?

81. By what description was singer Johnny Cash often referred to throughout his long and very successful career?

82. Who was the charismatic lead singer for the band Roxy Music who went on to have a successful solo career?

83. What was the late Dr. John's real name?

84. Which famous pop/rock star contributed backing vocals and instrumental support on "My Dark Hour" from the Steve Miller Band's 1969 album *Brave New World*?

85. Singer/songwriter and guitarist Richard Thompson was a member of which folk-rock group from Great Britain in the late '60s and early '70s?

86. Rock & roll pioneer and music icon Chuck Berry was originally from which Midwestern U.S. city?

87. Which famous record producer from the '60s and '70s was convicted of murder and died while serving time in prison?

88. Don McLean's song "American Pie" from the early '70s contains the lyrics "the day the music died." What event does this phrase refer to?

89. Which Bob Dylan album was released the following year after his 1966 motorcycle accident?

90. How did guitar wiz and blues-rock singer Stevie Ray Vaughan die?

91. Who was the guitarist for the '70s band Humble Pie, who went on to have his own very successful solo career?

92. "Not Fade Away" by Buddy Holly in the late '50s, "I Want Candy" by The Strangeloves in the '60s, and "Desire" by U2 in the '80s all contain a distinctive musical rhythm that is commonly called what?

93. The Commodores' 1985 hit song "Nightshift" pays tribute to which two great pop and soul artists?

94. Janis Joplin, Jimi Hendrix, and Jim Morrison all died at what age?

95. The 1990 hit record "Black Velvet" by Alannah Myles pays homage to which pop-rock icon and music pioneer?

96. In John Mellencamp's 1986 hit song "R.O.C.K. in the U.S.A.," he gives a few shoutouts to pop and soul stars from the '60s. Name the music acts Mellencamp refers to by name.

97. Rock pioneer Alice Cooper's father had a chosen calling that appeared to be in direct opposition to Alice's shock-rock persona. What did his father do?

Session 4: The Beatles

98. Which Beatles album was the first to be released on their own Apple Records label?

99. Before Linda Eastman met Paul McCartney and eventually became Linda McCartney, what was her profession at the time?

100. Name the world-famous singer who once said that, in his opinion, "Something" by The Beatles was one of the greatest love songs ever written.

101. What disease did Ringo have as a young child?

102. When The Beatles recruited Ringo to join the band, he was a drummer in another Liverpool band. Name that band.

103. Name the Beatles drummer that Ringo replaced.

104. Which Beatles song is the first to be credited as being written by all four band members?

The Fab Four were the first, and most groundbreaking, pop band that I embraced. They landed on our shores from England in the months following the 1963 JFK assassination. Our country needed cheering up, and their music gave us hope, inspiration, and a massive dose of Beatlemania.

105. Who was the oldest member of The Beatles?

106. Name the drummer who filled in for Ringo Starr on the Beatles' tour of Australia in 1964 when Ringo became sick with tonsillitis?

107. Who was the first American singer in the 1960s to record a cover version of a Beatles song?

108. Name the Beatles song that contains the lyrics, "Sunday's on the phone to Monday, Tuesday's on the phone to me."

109. Which Beatles band member quit the band briefly during the recording of "The White Album" in 1968 but returned a while later at the urgent requests of the other Beatles?

110. According to a very well-known No. 1 Beatles song from early 1965, how many days in a week?

111. "Lucy in the Sky With Diamonds" was written by John Lennon and first appeared on the album *Sgt. Pepper's Lonely Hearts Club Band* in 1967. John said his inspiration for the song came from a drawing by whom?

Session 5: Drummers

112. Let's play Name That Drummer! Who are, or were, the drummers for the following well-known and long-running rock bands from a variety of decades who helped propel their respective bands to great music industry success.

    a) Bon Jovi
    b) Aerosmith
    c) Red Hot Chili Peppers
    d) Van Halen
    e) Black Sabbath
    f) The White Stripes
    g) The Rolling Stones
    h) Cream
    i) Nirvana
    j) Foo Fighters
    k) Led Zeppelin
    l) Toto

Drumming has always been an important part of my musical journey. There are lots of competent drummers, and there are the truly great stick handlers who have propelled pop and rock forward with well-placed, memorable beats. I'm talking about Hal Blaine, Keith Moon, and John Bonham for starters. Drums are always the first thing I hear in a song.

m) Rush
n) The Dave Clark Five
o) Pink Floyd
p) The Police
q) Yes
r) The Jimi Hendrix Experience

113. Name the drummer who played on Paul McCartney's 1999 solo album *Run Devil, Run*, who was also the drummer in a very successful rock band throughout the '60s and '70s.

114. Name the studio session drummer who played on hundreds of hit records for various artists in the '60s and '70s and was a member of the talented collective of session musicians known as The Wrecking Crew.

115. Who was James Brown's drummer on the iconic and often-sampled 1969 tune "Funky Drummer"?

116. Name the rock drummer who played on just one album with Keith Emerson and Greg Lake in place of Carl Palmer in the mid-'80s.

Session 6: Songwriters

117. Name the famous and successful songwriters who wrote the No. 1 hit song "Raindrops Keep Falling On My Head." And can you name the blockbuster movie that featured this song?

118. Name the songwriting duo who wrote several great hit songs for The Monkees, including "Last Train To Clarksville" and *The Monkees* TV show theme song. And after launching their singing career as a duet, what was their biggest hit record?

119. Who wrote and recorded the first version of the iconic '60s song "Louie, Louie"?

120. Name the very famous singer-songwriter, who earlier in his career, wrote the following songs recorded by these artists in the '60s: "Bad To Me" – Billy J. Kramer; "A World Without Love" – Peter and Gordon; "Come and Get It" – Badfinger; "Goodbye" – Mary Hopkin.

I have great admiration for songwriters who express themselves so eloquently with music that becomes a part of our lives. Over the years, people like Smokey Robinson, Carole King, Leiber and Stoller, Mann and Weil, Holland-Dozier-Holland, Billy Joel, and Lennon and McCartney have all created magic with powerful and everlasting song craft.

121. Name the iconic singer-songwriter who wrote the '60s song "Gloria," and name the band he was in when they recorded the first version of this song.

122. Name each of the individual singer-songwriters who wrote the following two songs that were hits for Peter, Paul and Mary: "Early Mornin' Rain" and "Leaving On A Jet Plane."

123. Who wrote and recorded the original version of the well-known hit song "Summertime Blues"?

124. Little Eva recorded the '60s hit song "The Loco-Motion," written by Carole King and Gerry Goffin. How did the songwriters know Little Eva?

125. Which well-known children's author and humorist wrote the song "A Boy Named Sue," the 1969 hit record for Johnny Cash. And where was this hit song recorded?

126. Who co-wrote the Eagles' first hit song "Take It Easy" in the early '70s with Eagles band member Glenn Frey?

127. Name the singer-songwriter who wrote and originally recorded the song "Big Yellow Taxi" which was a hit again in the 2000s when Counting Crows covered it.

128. Who are "The Glimmer Twins"?

129. Which well-known, successful songwriting partners wrote the first hit song by Herman's Hermits, "I'm Into Something Good"?

Session 6: Songwriters

130. What did singer-songwriter Cat Stevens officially change his name to after his conversion to Islam?

131. Before the late Warren Zevon became a successful solo artist with "Werewolves of London," he wrote a song that was an early hit for the '60s band The Turtles. Name that song.

132. Who wrote the American opera *Porgy and Bess*? And name one of its most recognizable and often covered songs.

133. "And When I Die," "Eli's Coming," "Wedding Bell Blues," "Stoned Soul Picnic," and "Stoney End" are all songs written by which prolific songwriter of the '60s?

134. Patsy Cline's most popular and well-known hit song was "Crazy." Which country/pop singer and music icon wrote "Crazy"?

135. Before Linda Ronstadt became one of the most successful solo artists in music, she fronted a band called The Stone Poneys in the late '60s with a hit song, "Different Drum." Which member of a popular hit-making group from the '60s wrote "Different Drum"?

136. Who wrote the song "Nothing Compares 2 U" that was a big hit for Sinead O'Connor in the '90s? And what did she do after a performance on *Saturday Night Live* that created controversy?

137. Name the singer-songwriter who wrote one of the biggest and most popular Top 40 hits recorded by The Monkees, "Daydream Believer."

138. Which iconic American singer-songwriter co-wrote the 1960s hit song "Red Rubber Ball" that was a No. 2 hit for The Cyrkle?

139. "Red, Red Wine" was a big hit for the Jamaican pop group UB40 in the 1980s. Which well-known and very popular singer-songwriter wrote and recorded the original version in the '60s?

140. Name the songwriter who penned "For Your Love" and "Heart Full of Soul" by The Yardbirds and formed the very successful band 10cc in the 1980s.

141. "Wagon Wheel" was a hit record in 2013 for Darius Rucker, former lead singer of Hootie & the Blowfish. Which legendary singer-songwriter co-wrote this song?

142. Which songwriter wrote "Up, Up & Away" by The 5th Dimension, "By The Time I Get To Phoenix" and "Wichita Lineman" by Glen Campbell, and "MacArthur Park" by Richard Harris and later by Donna Summer?

143. With a successful career spanning several decades, which iconic pop music singer-songwriter is sometimes referred to as "The Belfast Cowboy"?

144. The 1986 No. 1 hit record for the band Heart, "These Dreams" was co-written by Elton John's longtime songwriting partner. Who is he?

145. Bobby Darin had a Top 10 hit in the mid-'60s with the song "If I Were a Carpenter." Which folk singer from that era wrote and recorded the original version?

Session 6: Songwriters

146. One of the Peter & Gordon hit records not written by Lennon and McCartney was "I Go To Pieces" from early 1965. Which popular American singer-songwriter, who also had hit records, wrote this song?

147. What do these artists, The Lettermen, Linda Ronstadt, Little Anthony & the Imperials, and songwriter-performer Bobby Hart (of Boyce & Hart), all have in common?

Session 7: Song Titles & Lyrics

Great songs or memorable lyrics are like special friends that really mean something to me - just like Shrevie in the 1982 movie, Diner. Imagine how boring music would be without great lyrics and catchy song titles!

148. What is the song title of the Bob Marley song that includes the following lyrics, "Don't worry about a thing, 'cause every little thing gonna be all right"?

149. Name the two members of the British government mentioned by their last names in the Beatles song "Taxman."

150. Name the cities mentioned in the song "Dancing in the Street," originally a hit for Martha and the Vandellas.

151. In the song "City of New Orleans," originally written and sung by Steve Goodman, how many "sacks of mail" are on the train?

152. The Elton John song "Candle in the Wind" had two versions released twenty-four years apart. Name the two iconic women who inspired each version of this song, the 1973 original and the 1997 reworked version.

153. Name a song that has a phone number in the song title.

154. Name a song that contains a time of day or night in the song title.

155. Name a song with the word "time" in the song title.

156. What is the shortest *Billboard* Hot 100 hit record?

157. What was the first No. 1 hit record on the U.S. *Billboard* Hot 100 by a British group?

158. What is the best-selling *Billboard* Top 10 hit record of the 1960s by a "one-hit wonder"?

159. What is the title of the classical composition commonly played at graduation ceremonies?

160. Name a pop song with the word "Joker" in the title.

161. Can you name some of the people that Paul McCartney name-checks in his song "Let 'Em In"?

162. In Rupert Holmes' 1979 hit record "Escape (The Piña Colada Song)," the song's main character is not into what and is into what?

163. Name the very well-known 1969 hit record that contains the following lyrics "I was raised by a toothless, bearded hag…"

164. The Aliotta, Haynes & Jeremiah hit song from the '70s "Lake Shore Drive" pays homage to a road in which U.S. city?

Session 7: Song Titles & Lyrics

165. Name the Beatles song that Johnny Rivers mentions by name in his 1967 hit song "Summer Rain."

166. What is the month and day sung in the opening line of Bobbie Gentry's No. 1 hit from 1967, "Ode To Billy Joe"?

167. Name the rock musician/singer-songwriter referred to in Lynyrd Skynyrd's classic hit "Sweet Home, Alabama."

168. In Roger Miller's hit song from the '60s "King of the Road," how much does it cost to rent a room? And what is his destination after hopping a freight train?

169. What is the connection between the 1967 hit song "Expressway To Your Heart" and the Steely Dan song "Hey Nineteen"?

170. Which popular song from the 1970s by Van Morrison used the made-up word "fantabulous" in the song lyrics?

171. According to the '70s Paul Simon song, name three ways to leave your lover.

Session 8: Record Albums

172. Track One – Side One. Name the first song on side one of the following debut albums: *The Doors*, *Are You Experienced* by The Jimi Hendrix Experience, and *Led Zeppelin*.

173. Which Rolling Stones album from the late '60s was their psychedelic answer to the Beatles album *Sgt. Pepper's Lonely Hearts Club Band*?

174. The rock band AC/DC hailed from which country? And name the best-selling and most well-known album in their catalog.

175. How many albums did Blind Faith record?

176. Name the album title by The Who that featured photos of the band members with various products – some real, some not.

177. Who was the studio engineer who worked on the Beatles album *Abbey Road* and the Pink Floyd album *Dark Side*

There are so many great songs, but putting together a truly great and inspiring record album is something to behold. The sequence of songs on an album side, and how they seem to flow into one another, is musical nirvana.

of the Moon, and also went on to form his own rock band that released a string of best-selling albums in the '70s and '80s?

178. Name the early '70s Jethro Tull album and title track about a homeless man in a public park.

179. Which '70s era Rolling Stones album was partly recorded at the famous Muscle Shoals recording studio in Alabama?

180. According to *Billboard* magazine, what is the best-selling pop/rock album of all time in the United States?

181. According to *Billboard* magazine, what is the best-selling pop/rock album of all time worldwide?

182. What was the title of the first Blood, Sweat & Tears album featuring lead singer and songwriter Al Kooper? And who replaced Al Kooper on lead vocals for the second BS&T album?

183. What was the title of the first solo album by a member of The Beatles?

184. What is the title of the long-awaited and somewhat controversial 2006 album by Guns N' Roses that was delayed several times by legal problems and personnel issues?

185. What was the title of Adele's best-selling album of 2011-2012 containing the hit songs "Rolling in the Deep" and "Someone like You"?

186. Pink Floyd's immensely successful '70s album *Dark Side of the Moon*

Session 8: Record Albums

spent several years on *Billboard's* top album chart and is one of the best-selling rock albums of all time. What iconic but understated graphic image is on this album's front cover?

187. Before punk rock pioneers The Clash had success with the songs "Rock the Casbah" and "Should I Stay or Should I Go," they released a momentous double album entitled what?

Session 10: Supergroups & Collaborations

What happens when you take great musicians from different bands and put them together to form a new band of blended talent? Often magic happens. I'm talking about The Traveling Wilburys, Asia, and Blind Faith to name a few.

189. Who were the four members of the late '60s supergroup Blind Faith?

190. Which bands were each of the members in before Blind Faith?

191. The Power Station was a supergroup with the 1985 hit song "Some Like It Hot." The Power Station's initial lead singer was Robert Palmer. On bass, lead guitar, and drums were members from which other successful bands?

192. Name the bands that Keith Emerson, Greg Lake, & Carl Palmer were in before forming Emerson, Lake & Palmer (ELP).

193. Name the pop/rock bands that each member of Crosby, Stills, Nash & Young were members of before teaming up to record together under CSNY.

194. Who did Danger Mouse team up with to form Gnarls Barkley

and record the Grammy-winning song "Crazy"?

195. Name the two rock superstars who collaborated in the early '70s in Derek and the Dominos. And what is the best-known classic rock song from this band that still gets radio airplay today?

196. In the late '70s, solo artists Dave Edmunds and Nick Lowe formed a band together featuring high-energy rockabilly and guitar-driven pop music. What was the band name of this collaboration?

197. The album *Super Session* released in 1968 was a collaboration of three well-known musicians from various bands. Who were they, and what was the connection one of these musicians had to the Chicago Blues scene at the time?

198. In 1978, singer-songwriter Dan Fogelberg teamed up with flutist Tim Weisberg to record a collaboration album with what title?

199. Name the two talented singer-musicians who in 1973 collaborated on one album before becoming an integral part of Fleetwood Mac.

200. Name the three members of the supergroup Cream.

201. The band Asia was a successful supergroup formed in the 1980s with members from which other well-known bands?

202. Name the superstar members of The Traveling Wilburys.

203. In the mid-'80s, members of several successful superstar rock bands, including Led Zeppelin and Bad Company, collaborated under what new band name?

Session 11: Record Labels

204. Name the record label that signed the following artists earlier in their careers: Van Morrison, Neil Diamond, and The McCoys.

205. Who was the first non-Beatles performer to release an album on the Beatles' newly-formed record label Apple Records?

206. Name the founder of Sun Records, responsible for producing many of Elvis Presley's early hits and who also brought together "The Million Dollar Quartet."

207. Name the pioneering blues and R&B record company founded by two brothers in Chicago that produced a wealth of great music in the '50s, '60s, and '70s. And name the two brothers.

208. Who was the founder and mastermind behind Motown Records?

I was a typical teenager consuming pop music on a variety of different record labels. Taking a pop song from concept to finished hit record used to be the exclusive domain of record labels and studios. That has changed with the rapid advancement of technology, but I still love to read record labels!

209. In the 1960s band known as The Mar-Keys, the musicians had an instrumental hit record with the song "Last Night." For which famous recording studio did these session musicians make hit records with various soul and R&B artists?

210. What was the first record released on the soon-to-be successful record label A&M Records?

211. Name the Chicago-based independent blues and jazz record label whose founder also had a Chicago record store for many years known as the Jazz Record Mart.

212. Name the early Rolling Stones song that paid homage to the famous, but now defunct, Chess Records.

Session 12: Radio, TV & Movies

213. Name the pop music TV show from the '60s that was a Dick Clark Production (not *American Bandstand*) and featured Paul Revere & the Raiders in an outdoor beach setting.

214. Which popular singer from the '60s sang the theme song for the TV show in the question above and had a hit record with it?

215. In the movie version of the rock opera *Tommy*, which famous and successful singer played the role of the Acid Queen?

216. Which well-known '60s rock band performed live on *The Smothers Brothers Comedy Hour* and caused an explosion in the studio resulting in a delayed return from a commercial break?

217. Name the pop music duo whose song "I'll Be There For You" became the well-known theme song for the

Some truly amazing synergies have happened in the media over the years. A relatively unknown song gets used in a blockbuster movie and the song becomes a massive hit. Or a familiar song is used in a new context on TV to create the perfect mood. And radio has introduced us to much of this great music over the years.

TV show *Friends*.

218. Chris Robinson, the lead singer of the rock band The Black Crowes, was married to which *Almost Famous* movie star? And who is her famous movie star mother?

219. *Viva Las Vegas* and *Blue Hawaii* are just two well-known movies starring which iconic pop star?

220. Who directed The Beatles in their first feature-length movie *A Hard Day's Night*, and also directed their second movie *Help!*?

221. What was the working title of the Beatles' second movie *Help!* prior to its release in movie theaters?

222. Female rock pioneer Suzi Quattro had a recurring acting role in the late '70s on which long-running American TV sitcom? And what was her character's name on the show?

223. Name the title of the mid-'80s movie that presented a fictionalized version of Mozart's life story starring Tom Hulce as Mozart.

224. What was the title of the 1987 movie documentary that celebrated the late Chuck Berry's 60th birthday?

225. In the movie *2001: A Space Odyssey*, director Stanley Kubrick paired classical music with scenes of outer space. Whose well-known waltz music was used in the movie? Name the title of the most recognizable waltz used in this film.

Session 12: Radio, TV & Movies

226. Which '80s pop star makes a brief cameo appearance in a non-singing role in the blockbuster movie *Back to the Future*?

227. Which late '60s hit movie featured the Simon & Garfunkel song "Mrs. Robinson"?

228. In what year did Casey Kasem's *American Top 40* radio show debut?

229. In the '70s, singer James Taylor teamed up with Dennis Wilson of The Beach Boys to make a feature-length road movie titled what?

230. According to *Billboard* magazine, what is the best-selling movie soundtrack of all time?

231. Name a non-Beatles movie in which Ringo Starr had an acting role.

232. Name the actress Ringo Starr met on the set of one of his movie acting roles and whom he eventually married.

233. Which nationally syndicated radio host signed off each of his shows with: "Keep your feet on the ground and keep reaching for the stars"?

234. Dusty Springfield's hit song from the '60s, "Son-of-a Preacher Man," got a new life when it was featured in which popular movie from the 1990s?

Session 13: Music Venues & Festivals

235. Name a band or solo performer who appeared at the first Woodstock Music & Art Fair in August of 1969.

236. Name the race track/speedway in California where The Rolling Stones held a concert, and a concert-goer was stabbed to death.

237. And who did The Rolling Stones hire to provide security for the concert mentioned in the previous question?

238. Name the big music festival that took place in California two years before the 1969 Woodstock Music & Art Fair in New York.

239. Name the Hollywood music club where many great artists performed in the '60s and '70s, and where Johnny Rivers recorded several hit records in a live setting.

240. Name the theater and city where "Fingertips," the 1963 live performance of Little Stevie Wonder's first hit record,

I went to a lot of concerts and festivals growing up, with exposure to a wide variety of musical venues in Chicago and elsewhere. Each live music performance is unique, and the shared experience with fellow music lovers can be life-affirming.

was recorded.

241. The famous New York City nightclub CBGB became the cultural epicenter for punk and new wave music and bands in the '70s. What do the initials CBGB stand for?

Session 14: Sports + Music = Fun

242. The No. 1 hit record from 1969, "Na Na Hey Hey Kiss Him Goodbye," became a theme song for which Major League Baseball team nearly a decade later?

243. Who wrote and recorded the song "Go Cubs, Go" that is still played at Wrigley Field in Chicago?

244. Name the song used during player introductions at Chicago Bulls home basketball games in the Michael Jordan era.

245. Which well-known and popular '70s era sing-a-long dance track is frequently played at sports stadiums?

246. Name the two American cities in the lyrics of the classic baseball song "It's a Beautiful Day For a Ballgame."

247. Which rock song with alternating foot stomping and hand clapping has become a stadium anthem at sporting events worldwide?

So you're at a baseball game, or a hockey game, or a rugby match. Keeping you entertained at the event are stadium-worthy rock anthems and fun sing-a-longs! I wonder if Freddie Mercury of Queen and members of The Village People could have ever imagined their music playing at sporting events many decades in the future!

248. "Hey! Baby" is frequently played at a variety of sporting events. Who had the original No. 1 hit record back in 1962?

Session 15: Classical

249. Name a well-known Mozart symphony that shares its name with a planet in our solar system.

250. Who composed the widely known classical music suite "The Four Seasons"?

251. Which prolific composer did rock pioneer Chuck Berry specifically call out by name in one of his songs?

252. Name one of the most recognizable Beethoven symphonies based on the opening four notes - "da-da-da-dum."

253. What is the middle name of one of the greatest composers of all time, Johann Bach?

254. Which prolific composer, considered to be the father of symphonic music and string quartets, was Beethoven's tutor and Mozart's mentor?

Mozart, Bach, Beethoven, and Haydn were the original pop stars. Elton John dressed in the period garb of the 1700s when he performed an amazing live version of "Candle in the Wind." And Chuck Berry even told Beethoven to roll over!

Session 16: Jazz & Blues

255. Name the late Chicago blues singer and prolific songwriter who wrote many great blues songs including "Can't Judge a Book By the Cover," "Spoonful," "You Shook Me," "Little Red Rooster," and "The Seventh Son."

256. Name the legendary Delta Blues pioneer from the 1930s who wrote songs covered decades later by various rock and blues artists. Among his best-known songs are "Sweet Home Chicago," "Crossroads," and "Love in Vain."

257. Rock and blues performers, including The Animals and Big Head Todd and the Monsters, covered the blues standard "Boom Boom." Who wrote and recorded the original version?

258. The late, great bluesman Muddy Waters billed himself with the name of which U.S. state on his 1979 live album?

My musical palette expanded in college to include jazz and blues, considered by many to be the purest forms of uniquely American music. The Brits listened intently to American Rhythm and Blues, and they tossed amped-up blues-rock back over the pond to us via The Yardbirds, The Animals, The Rolling Stones, and Led Zeppelin.

259. The late blues icon B.B. King gave all of his Gibson guitars the same female name. What did he name his guitars?

260. Known for their high-energy, up-tempo blues-rock records and performances, what menacing name did George Thorogood give his backing band?

261. Which iconic album is often touted as the best-selling jazz album of all time?

262. Name a well-known Duke Ellington jazz composition that contains both a type of fabric and a type of toy in the title.

263. Name the original members of The Modern Jazz Quartet.

264. The late Toots Thielemans is renowned in jazz, easy listening, and movie theme music for which instrument?

265. What was the title of the Miles Davis album that ushered in a new era of post-bebop jazz in the late '50s?

266. According to the title of a popular Duke Ellington Orchestra song, which train should you take?

Session 17: Rap & Hip Hop

267. Which hip hop trio's rap song was the first to reach *Billboard's* Top 40?

268. Which female artist was the first to receive ten nominations and five awards at the 41st Grammy Awards in 1999?

269. Who recorded a rap version of Aerosmith's "Walk This Way"?

270. Name the No. 1 pop song from the early '80s that was the first to feature rap vocals and name the band that recorded it.

271. What is the name of the hip hop record label started by rap artist Jay-Z in 1995?

272. Which New York hip hop group collaborated with The Beach Boys in the late '80s on a very different version of the '60s surf song "Wipeout"?

If only the beatniks of the late 1950s could have known how spoken word expressions and beat poetry would evolve into unstoppable forces of creativity in our musical evolution.

Session 18: Musical Instruments

273. What is the only acoustic instrument invented in the 20th Century?

274. Which brass instrument is prominently featured on the opening track "Overture" on the rock opera album *Tommy* by The Who?

275. Wendy Carlos pioneered the use of which electronic instrument in classical music?

276. What type of horn does jazz and easy listening music superstar Chuck Mangione play on his records and in concert?

277. Which keyboard instrument, commonly heard in classical music, was used in the Rolling Stones song "Lady Jane"?

I always want to know how a unique or unusual sound in a pop song is generated. The advent of electronics in music has had a profound effect on expanding our pallet of options and effects. The Beach Boys using a Theremin in the song, "Good Vibrations," was an early example.

278. In much of their music, The Moody Blues utilized an electro-mechanical keyboard instrument that mimics an orchestral sound using magnetic tape, capstans, and playback heads. What is this instrument called?

279. Which '60s era American folk-rock band pioneered using the Rickenbacker electric 12-string guitar?

Session 19: THE 1960s

My favorite musical decade from my teen years! The explosion of pop and rock groups and songwriting creativity in the '60s, along with the dawning of the sexual revolution, created some of the most memorable music in history.

280. The 1966 hit song "Dirty Water" by The Standells became an anthem for which U.S. city? Which river in that city is mentioned by name in the song?

281. Name the singing group from the early '60s that recorded the original hit "Do You Love Me," later covered by The Dave Clark Five. And what blockbuster movie featured the song?

282. Name a Top 40 pop group that hailed from the Chicago area during the 1960s.

283. Name the only No. 1 hit in the U.S. by The Turtles.

284. Name the famous area in San Francisco that became the epicenter of the psychedelic music and hippy culture during 1967's "Summer of Love."

285. Name the pop singer who sang the '60s hit "The Last Waltz."

286. According to music industry statistics, which significant

hit record from the mid-'60s became the most-played record of the 20th Century?

287. Name the Elvis sound-alike singer who had a bigger hit with the song "Suspicion" than the original by Elvis Presley.

288. Name a classic surf music instrumental hit from the early '60s that still gets radio airplay on oldies radio stations.

289. Frank Sinatra and his daughter Nancy recorded a duet in the '60s that became a No. 1 hit record. What was the title of the song?

290. Who was one of the first well-known comedians to have a Top 40 hit record in 1967 on the *Billboard* charts?

291. Which pop song from the 1960s was the first to use guitar feedback as part of the introduction?

292. American singer/songwriter John D. Loudermilk wrote many great songs in the '60s, including "Tobacco Road" and "Indian Reservation." He also wrote "Then You Can Tell Me Goodbye." Name the pop group that reached No. 6 on the *Billboard* charts in 1967 with this song.

293. Scottish-born singer-songwriter Donovan Leitch, simply known as Donovan, had only one No. 1 record on the U.S. *Billboard* Hot 100. Name this song from the mid-'60s.

294. Which protest song from the mid-'60s played a role in the U.S. government lowering the national voting age from twenty-one to eighteen?

Session 20: The 1970s

295. Name the singing group who recorded the '70s hit song "Afternoon Delight." And which famous folk singer were they friends with at the time?

296. Name the artist whose mid-'70s hit record "Convoy" capitalized on the CB Radio craze of the time.

297. Who sang the '70s monster hit "I Will Survive"?

298. Which hit song written and sung by Randy Newman in the late '70s caused a backlash despite being a tongue-in-cheek take on a specific group of people?

299. What was the song title of the hit record from Todd Rundgren's second band that reached *Billboard's* Top 20 in 1971?

300. Andrew Gold had a Top 10 hit record with the song "Lonely Boy" in 1977. What was his connection to Linda Ronstadt and the long-running American TV sitcom *The Golden Girls*?

301. Ringo Starr's first solo hit record after the Beatles' break-up was "It Don't Come Easy." Who wrote this song with Ringo?

The '70s were all over the place musically. Funk, punk, disco, hard rock, and cheesy pop hits were all on display in this "wild and crazy" decade.

Session 21: The 1980s & Beyond

302. The R.E.M. song "What's the Frequency, Kenneth?" refers to which American TV news journalist and anchorman?

303. The rock band Golden Earring had a hit record in the '70s with "Radar Love." Name an '80s U.S. hit song by Golden Earring with a slower tempo and very different sound.

304. The '80s band 'Til Tuesday had a hit record with the song "Voices Carry" in 1985. Name the female lead singer of this band who went on to have a successful solo career.

305. Singer-songwriter Michael Penn, actor Sean Penn's younger brother, had a Top 20 hit record in 1989 with which song?

306. What is hanging out of the back pocket of Bruce Springsteen's jeans on the cover of his iconic 1984 album *Born in the U.S.A.*?

Bad haircuts and oversized clothing with big shoulder pads were not the only highlights of the '80s. We also had Duran Duran, R.E.M., and U2, followed by grunge, screamo, and emo in the '90s. These were major musical transitions from previous decades!

307. Name the rock group that sang the song from the late '90s "Breakfast at Tiffany's."

308. Producer, songwriter, and performer Brian Burton, aka Danger Mouse, mashed up music from the Beatles "White Album" with songs from Jay-Z's *The Black Album* in 2003. What is the title of this mash-up by Danger Mouse?

309. What was Natalie Imbruglia's career before becoming a pop star in the late '90s with the hit song "Torn"?

310. Which '90s rock band had a song "Can't Hardly Wait" that inspired the title of a late '90s film with the same name?

Session 22: Copycats

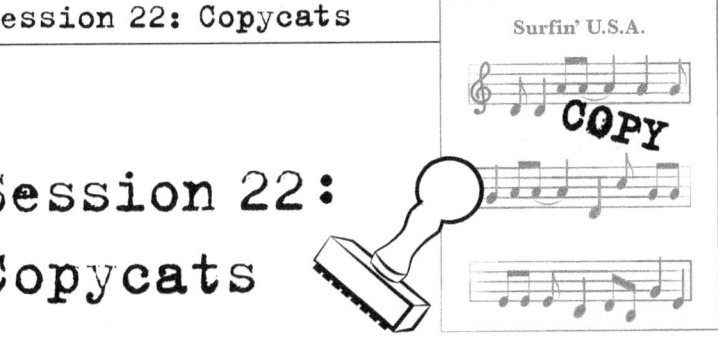

311. The Beach Boys song "Be True To Your School" contains a melody from which university fight song played briefly on the keyboard during the song's instrumental part?

312. Which iconic singer-songwriter/guitarist sued The Beach Boys for songwriting royalties on "Surfin' U.S.A.," and which song did it copy?

313. George Harrison was successfully sued for copyright infringement on one of his biggest solo hits. Name the early '70s Harrison song and the original '60s song at the center of the litigation.

314. What was the title of Jody Miller's female answer song to Roger Miller's "King of the Road"?

315. What is the connection between the mid-'60s Kinks song "All Day and All of the Night" and the early '70s Doors song "Hello, I Love You"?

Copying is said to be the highest form of flattery, but that's not always true in the world of music. Sometimes similarities in pop songs are astounding and result in lawsuits, and sometimes they're just barely similar. There are many examples of frequently-copied chord progressions, or sampled guitar riffs, that have been used in pop songs in new and interesting ways.

316. The piano intro to the 1968 hit record "The Ballad of Bonnie and Clyde" by Georgie Fame imitates the piano intro of which Fats Domino song from the late '50s?

317. And finally...the musical intro of the Steely Dan song "Rikki Don't Lose That Number" is the same intro as which instrumental jazz standard by Horace Silver?

Trivia Jam Answers

Session 1: Band Names & Personnel

1. The New Yardbirds. Guitarist Jimmy Page was the only member of the original Yardbirds who went on to form The New Yardbirds that became Led Zeppelin.
2. The Hawks. They became simply The Hawks after parting ways with Ronnie Hawkins when the group was called Ronnie Hawkins and the Hawks.
3. Rod Argent. "Hold Your Head Up" by Argent.
4. Jim Messina was in Poco before joining up with Kenny Loggins.
5. Bachman-Turner Overdrive. "You Ain't Seen Nothing Yet" and "Takin' Care of Business" were their highest-charting hit records on the *Billboard* Hot 100.
6. Flo & Eddie
7. Grace Slick was the lead singer for much of the band's history and several band name changes. She was a member of the band The Great Society before joining Jefferson Airplane.
8. The First Edition. They later became Kenny Rogers & The First Edition. "Just Dropped In (To See What Condition My Condition Was In)" was their first hit.
9. Mountain – lead by guitarist and vocalist Leslie West
10. New Rhythm and Blues Quartet

11. Despite popular belief, Bee Gees is not a direct reference to Brothers Gibb. The name originated from the initials of two individuals who were instrumental in promoting the early group, along with band member Barry Gibb, who all had the same initials, B.G.

12. Before going solo, Todd Rundgren was in two different bands – The Nazz and Runt.

13. Lighthouse. The two bands were Lighthouse and Edison Lighthouse, respectively.

14. Here's a few: Kansas; Little Texas; Alabama; Hannah Montana; Florida Georgia Line; North Mississippi Allstars.

15. ZZ Top

16. The Fabulous Thunderbirds

17. Gerry Rafferty was in Stealers Wheel, and their top 10 record from 1973 was "Stuck in the Middle with You."

18. Curtis Mayfield was a member of the Impressions. The great Chicago soul singer Jerry Butler was also a member of the Impressions.

19. Joe Walsh led the early '70s band The James Gang.

20. The Finn Brothers are from New Zealand, and "I Got You" was by Split Enz.

21. War

22. DePaul University in Chicago

23. Ray and Dave Davies

24. Jerry Garcia, Phil Lesh, Bill Kreutzmann, Bob Weir, and Ron "Pigpen" McKernan

Answers: Session 1

were the original members of the Grateful Dead. Mickey Hart and Robert Hunter joined the band very early on and were also core members of the Grateful Dead.

25. Elvis Presley's drummer was D.J. Fontana, and his guitar player was Scotty Moore. These great musicians did not get all the recognition they deserved for their contributions.

26. The Kinks – brothers Dave and Ray Davies; Oasis – Noel and Liam Gallagher; Hanson – Taylor, Zac, and Isaac Hanson; Jonas Brothers – Joe, Nick, and Kevin Jonas, are just a few examples.

27. Walter Becker and Donald Fagen. The band's name was inspired by an adult-oriented product mentioned in the William S. Burroughs novel *Naked Lunch*.

28. Jim Seals of Seals & Crofts and "England Dan" Seals were brothers.

29. Carnie and Wendy Wilson are the daughters of Brian Wilson from The Beach Boys. Chynna Phillips is the daughter of John and Michelle Phillips of The Mamas & the Papas.

30. The Blossoms

31. The only surviving member of the Bee Gees is Barry Gibb. Gibb brothers Robin and Maurice are no longer with us (or the group).

32. Son Volt (Jay Farrar) and Wilco (Jeff Tweedy)

33. Skunk Baxter was a member of The Doobie Brothers.

34. Sylvia Robinson was a member of the '50s duo Mickey & Sylvia ("Love Is Strange").

35. Dave Mason wrote "Feelin' Alright" when he was a member of Traffic.
36. The female backing singers for Ray Charles were The Raelettes.
37. Todd Rundgren, Gregg Rolie (Santana), Steve Lukather (Toto), Gregg Bissonette (session drummer), Jim Keltner (drummer for several artists from Ringo to George Harrison to the Traveling Wilburys), and Nils Lofgren (Bruce Springsteen's E Street Band and solo artist) just to name a few.

Session 2: Cover Versions & Originals

38. "Money (That's What I Want)." It was originally a hit by Barrett Strong.
39. The original artists on various songs covered by The Beatles:
    a) "Act Naturally" Buck Owens
    b) "Boys" The Shirelles
    c) "Roll Over Beethoven" Chuck Berry
    d) "Dizzy, Miss Lizzy" Larry Williams
    e) "Twist and Shout" The Top Notes, later covered more successfully by The Isley Brothers
    f) "Please Mr. Postman" The Marvelettes
40. Fleetwood Mac
41. Dale Hawkins
42. Commander Cody and His Lost Planet Airmen
43. J. Frank Wilson and the Cavaliers

Answers: Sessions 1 & 2

44. "Fire"
45. David Bowie
46. Bananarama
47. Bruce Springsteen wrote "Blinded By The Light" and recorded the original version before Manfred Mann's cover.
48. Smiley Lewis, a New Orleans R&B performer, had the original hit with the song "I Hear You Knocking."
49. The rock band Weezer recorded a successful cover of "Africa."
50. Johnny Winter first recorded "Rock and Roll, Hoochie Koo."
51. British singer Don Fardon
52. Johnny Burnette
53. "I Wanna Be Your Man" written by Lennon-McCartney
54. Big Mama Thornton
55. Marvin Gaye's version reached No. 1 on the *Billboard* Hot 100. Gladys Knight & the Pips and Creedence Clearwater Revival also charted with their covers.
56. Brenda Holloway
57. The original version was by The Crickets, but the highest-charting version was by The Bobby Fuller Four in 1966. The Clash and Green Day also had well-known covers of the song.
58. Nina Simone

59. Rita Coolidge remade Jackie Wilson's song as "(Your Love Has Lifted Me) Higher and Higher" in 1977.
60. "Lookin' for a Love" was covered in the early '70s by The J. Geils Band.
61. "Superman" was originally recorded by The Clique in 1969.
62. The Tremeloes

Session 3: Performers & Pioneers

63. Simon & Garfunkel originally called themselves Tom & Jerry.
64. Johnny Cash, Elvis Presley, Jerry Lee Lewis, and Carl Perkins made up "The Million Dollar Quartet."
65. Lead guitarist/vocalist Terry Kath
66. Eric Clapton, Jimmy Page, and Jeff Beck
67. Steve Cropper - guitarist, writer, and arranger at Stax Recording Studio in Memphis. He was also a member of Booker T. & the M.G.'s ("Green Onions") and the Blues Brothers backing band in the movie, on records, and in concert.
68. Michael Jackson
69. The Wrecking Crew
70. Paul McCartney
71. Johnny Cash recorded the duet "Girl from the North Country" with Bob Dylan on *Nashville Skyline*.

Answers: Sessions 2 & 3

72. Ian Anderson, who played flute – unusual for the leader of a rock band
73. Drummer, percussionist, and singer Sheila E.
74. Elton John
75. Merry Clayton sang the very emotional backing vocal on "Gimme Shelter."
76. Paul Rodgers was the lead singer for the band Free and later went on to form the rock band Bad Company.
77. Neil Diamond
78. Chrissie Hynde of The Pretenders had a daughter with Ray Davies of The Kinks in 1983, but the relationship ended, and Chrissie later married Jim Kerr of the band Simple Minds.
79. Livingston Taylor
80. "You're No Good" was Linda Ronstadt's only No. 1 record, despite her overwhelming popularity and multi-decade success as one of the most popular female vocalists of all time.
81. Johnny Cash was often referred to as "The Man in Black" because of his fondness for dressing in black for performances.
82. Bryan Ferry
83. Malcolm John Rebennack Jr., also known as Mac Rebennack
84. Paul McCartney, credited on the album as Paul Ramon
85. Richard Thompson was a co-founder and member of the folk-rock band Fairport Convention.

86. St. Louis

87. Phil Spector

88. "The day the music died" refers to the February 1959 plane crash that killed Buddy Holly, Ritchie Valens, and The Big Bopper.

89. Bob Dylan's album *John Wesley Harding,* released in 1967

90. A helicopter crash after a concert in Wisconsin

91. Peter Frampton

92. These three songs and many more are examples of the "Bo Diddley Beat."

93. "Nightshift" by The Commodores pays tribute to Jackie Wilson and Marvin Gaye.

94. Janis Joplin, Jimi Hendrix, and Jim Morrison all died at age 27.

95. "Black Velvet" by Alannah Myles pays homage to Elvis Presley, whose image was often portrayed in black velvet paintings.

96. John Mellencamp's "R.O.C.K. in the U.S.A." gives shoutouts to Frankie Lyman, Mitch Ryder, Jackie Wilson, Bobby Fuller, The Young Rascals, The Shangri-Las, Martha Reeves, and James Brown.

97. Alice Cooper's father was an evangelist in The Church of Jesus Christ, and his grandfather was also deeply involved in the same church.

Answers: Sessions 3 & 4

Session 4: The Beatles

98. Commonly referred to as "The White Album," *The Beatles* was the first Beatles album on Apple Records.
99. Linda Eastman was a photographer.
100. Frank Sinatra, who regularly performed "Something" in concert
101. Ringo had tuberculosis as a young boy.
102. Rory Storm and the Hurricanes
103. Pete Best
104. The instrumental "Flying" from the Beatles album *Magical Mystery Tour*
105. Ringo Starr was born in July 1940, just a few months before John Lennon.
106. British drummer Jimmie Nicol filled in for Ringo on eight of the Beatles' tour appearances until Ringo was well enough to rejoin the band in Australia.
107. Del Shannon. He covered "From Me To You" in 1963.
108. "She Came in Through the Bathroom Window" from the Beatles album *Abbey Road*.
109. Ringo Starr. The other band members welcomed him back with flowers on his drum kit.
110. "Eight Days a Week"
111. The inspiration for "Lucy in the Sky With Diamonds" was a drawing by John's three-year-old son Julian.

Session 5: Drummers

112. Here are the answers to Name That Drummer:
    a) Bon Jovi - Tico Torres
    b) Aerosmith - Joey Kramer
    c) Red Hot Chili Peppers - Chad Smith
    d) Van Halen - Alex Van Halen
    e) Black Sabbath - Bill Ward
    f) The White Stripes - Meg White
    g) The Rolling Stones - Charlie Watts
    h) Cream - Ginger Baker
    i) Nirvana - Dave Grohl
    j) Foo Fighters - Taylor Hawkins
    k) Led Zeppelin - John Bonham
    l) Toto - Jeff Porcaro
    m) Rush - Neil Peart
    n) The Dave Clark Five - Dave Clark
    o) Pink Floyd - Nick Mason
    p) The Police - Stewart Copeland
    q) Yes - initially, Bill Bruford then Alan White since 2015
    r) The Jimi Hendrix Experience - Mitch Mitchell

113. Drummer Ian Paice played on Paul's album and was also the longtime drummer for the band Deep Purple.

114. Hal Blaine

Answers: Sessions 5 & 6

115. Clyde Stubblefield
116. Cozy Powell. The album title was *Emerson, Lake & Powell*.

Session 6: Songwriters

117. Burt Bachrach and Hal David. And the movie was *Butch Cassidy and the Sundance Kid*.
118. Tommy Boyce and Bobby Hart. Their biggest hit under their duet name Boyce and Hart was "I Wonder What She's Doing Tonight."
119. Richard Berry wrote the song and recorded an early version of "Louie Louie" with his band The Pharaohs. The Kingsmen had the biggest hit version, reaching No. 2 on the *Billboard* Hot 100 in 1963 and No. 97 in 1966.
120. Paul McCartney wrote or co-wrote all of these songs. "Bad to Me" and "A World Without Love" were credited to Lennon-McCartney.
121. Van Morrison. He was in the band known as Them when he wrote "Gloria."
122. Gordon Lightfoot and John Denver, respectively
123. Eddie Cochran. "Summertime Blues" has been covered by many bands over the years, including The Who. The hard rock band Blue Cheer also had a Top 20 hit with this song in 1968.
124. Little Eva was their babysitter.
125. Shel Silverstein. "A Boy Named Sue" was recorded at a live concert Johnny Cash gave at San Quentin State Prison in California.

126. Jackson Browne co-wrote "Take It Easy" with Glenn Frey of The Eagles. Jackson Browne also recorded his own version of the song.

127. Joni Mitchell

128. The Rolling Stones songwriting duo of Mick Jagger and Keith Richards

129. Carole King and Gerry Goffin

130. Yusuf Islam. He calls himself simply Yusuf on his more recent recordings.

131. "Outside Chance" by The Turtles

132. George Gershwin wrote *Porgy and Bess,* and "Summertime" is one of its most recognizable and often-covered songs.

133. Laura Nyro. She wrote hit songs for artists including Three Dog Night, The 5th Dimension, and Blood, Sweat & Tears.

134. Willie Nelson

135. Michael Nesmith of The Monkees

136. Prince wrote "Nothing Compares 2 U." Singer Sinead O'Connor appeared on *SNL* in 1992 and concluded her performance by tearing up a color photo of Pope John Paul II as a statement against sexual abuse in the Catholic Church.

137. John Stewart wrote "Daydream Believer," which became a No. 1 hit song for The Monkees in 1967.

138. Paul Simon

139. Neil Diamond

Answers: Sessions 6 & 7

140. Graham Gouldman
141. Bob Dylan
142. Jimmy Webb
143. Van Morrison, also referred to as "Van the Man"
144. "These Dreams" was co-written by Elton John's songwriting partner Bernie Taupin.
145. The late Tim Hardin wrote Bobby Darin's hit "If I Were a Carpenter." The Four Tops also recorded the song.
146. Peter & Gordon's "I Go To Pieces" was written by Del Shannon.
147. Bobby Hart co-wrote the classic song "Hurts So Bad." It has been covered by various artists, including Linda Ronstadt, The Lettermen, and Little Anthony & the Imperials, with the first big hit version.

Session 7: Song Titles & Lyrics

148. "Three Little Birds"
149. Mr. Wilson and Mr. Heath, both members of the British government, were called out in the song "Taxman."
150. Chicago, New Orleans, New York City, Philadelphia, Baltimore, D.C., The Motor City (Detroit), and L.A. are all cities mentioned in this song.
151. There were "three conductors and 25 sacks of mail" on board the City of New Orleans in Steve Goodman's song.

152. The 1973 original version of "Candle in the Wind" was about iconic movie star Marilyn Monroe. The 1997 modified version was a tribute to England's Princess Diana following her death.

153. Wilson Pickett's "634-5789", Tommy Tutone's "867-5309/Jenny", Glen Miller's "Pennsylvania 6-5000", and The Marvelettes' "Beechwood 4-5789" are all possible answers.

154. "3 A.M. Eternal" by The KLF, "It's 2 A.M." by Shemekia Copeland, "Six O'Clock" by The Lovin' Spoonful, and "Twelve Thirty" by The Mamas and the Papas are all possible answers.

155. Here are just a few – "Time Won't Let Me" by The Outsiders, "Time Has Come Today" by The Chambers Brothers, "Time Is On My Side" and "Last Time" by The Rolling Stones, and "Does Anyone Really Know What Time It Is?" by Chicago.

156. "Stay" by Maurice Williams and the Zodiacs at only 1 minute, 36 seconds long.

157. The first record by a British group to hit No. 1 on the U.S. charts was "Telstar" by The Tornados in December 1962. The first British recording to reach No. 1 in the U.S. was "Stranger on the Shore" by Mr. Acker Bilk, backed by the Leon Young String Chorale in May 1962.

158. The instrumental "Love Is Blue" by Paul Mauriat in 1968

159. "Pomp and Circumstance" by Edward Elgar

160. "The Joker Went Wild" by Brian Hyland, "The Joker" by The Steve Miller Band, and "Jokerman" by Bob Dylan are possible answers.

Answers: Session 7

161. Phil & Don (The Everly Brothers), McCartney's Auntie Gin and his brother Michael, Martin Luther (priest, author, and reformation leader), and Uncle Ernie (a character in the rock opera *Tommy* by The Who)

162. In "Escape (The Piña Colada Song)," the main character is *not* "much into health food" and *is* "into champagne."

163. "Jumpin' Jack Flash" by The Rolling Stones

164. "Lake Shore Drive" is about the road that runs along Lake Michigan in Chicago from the north end of the city to the south.

165. Johnny Rivers name-drops the Beatles song "Sgt. Pepper's Lonely Hearts Club Band" in his song "Summer Rain."

166. "It was the 3rd of June, another sleepy, dusty delta day…"

167. Neil Young, as a result of Neil's less-than-flattering characterization of southern attitudes and beliefs in his song "Southern Man."

168. Fifty cents to rent a room, and he hopped a midnight freight train heading to Bangor, Maine.

169. The 1967 hit "Expressway To Your Heart" was by The Soul Survivors. Steely Dan's song "Hey Nineteen" specifically mentions this band's name.

170. "Moondance" by Van Morrison

171. According to Paul Simon, here are three ways out of "50 Ways to Leave Your Lover": "slip out the back, Jack;" "hop on the bus, Gus;" and "just drop off the key, Lee."

Session 8: Record Albums

172. Track One - Side One:
    The Doors - "Break On Through (To The Other Side),"
    Are You Experienced - "Purple Haze,"
    Led Zeppelin - "Good Times, Bad Times"

173. *Their Satanic Majesties Request* was the Rolling Stones album with a psychedelic sound and an album cover that mimicked the Beatles' *Sgt. Pepper* album.

174. Australia. AC/DC's album *Back in Black* is, according to *Billboard*, one of the best-selling rock albums of all time.

175. Just one album, simply titled *Blind Faith*

176. *The Who Sell Out*

177. Alan Parsons, who also formed The Alan Parsons Project.

178. The album and song are both titled *Aqualung*.

179. *Sticky Fingers* by The Rolling Stones

180. *The Eagles Greatest Hits 1971-1975*

181. *Thriller* by Michael Jackson

182. The first album by Blood, Sweat & Tears was titled *Child Is Father to the Man*. That album featured singer-songwriter Al Kooper who left the group after the first album. The band recruited Canadian singer-songwriter David Clayton-Thomas as the lead singer for their second and very successful self-titled album *Blood, Sweat & Tears*.

Answers: Session 8 & 9

183. *Wonderwall Music* by George Harrison, which was also the first album released on the Apple Records label

184. *Chinese Democracy*

185. Adele's best-selling album of 2011-2012 was titled *21*.

186. Pink Floyd's *Dark Side of the Moon* features a simple graphic image of light passing through a prism on the album's front cover.

187. *London Calling* by The Clash, one of *Rolling Stone's* 500 Greatest Albums of All Time

Session 9: Flip Sides

188. Pop Music Flip Sides:
    a) "Act Naturally" ("Yesterday")
    b) "Stupid Girl" ("Paint It Black")
    c) "I'm Free" ("Get Off My Cloud")
    d) "Yellow Submarine" ("Eleanor Rigby")
    e) "What Goes On" ("Nowhere Man")
    f) "Rain" ("Paperback Writer")
    g) "We Can Work It Out" ("Day Tripper")
    h) "Revolution" ("Hey Jude")
    i) "Let's Go Away For Awhile" ("Good Vibrations")
    j) "The Crystal Ship" ("Light My Fire")
    k) "God Only Knows" ("Wouldn't It Be Nice")

l) "The Under Assistant West Coast Promotion Man" ("(I Can't Get No) Satisfaction")

m) "The Wind Cries Mary" ("Purple Haze")

Session 10: Supergroups & Collaborations

189. Eric Clapton, Ginger Baker, Steve Winwood, and Ric Grech

190. Eric Clapton and Ginger Baker were in Cream, Steve Winwood had been in The Spencer Davis Group and Traffic, and Ric Grech was in Family.

191. The Power Station's bass and lead guitarists John and Andy Taylor were from Duran Duran, and the drummer Tony Thompson was a member of the band Chic.

192. Keith Emerson was in The Nice, Greg Lake was in King Crimson, and Carl Palmer was in Atomic Rooster before ELP.

193. David Crosby was in The Byrds, Stephen Stills and Neil Young were in Buffalo Springfield, and Graham Nash was in The Hollies.

194. CeeLo Green

195. Guitar wiz Duane Allman teamed up with guitar icon Eric Clapton in Derek and the Dominos. "Layla" is the classic rock song from this collaboration that is considered one of the greatest rock songs of all time.

196. Rockpile

197. Mike Bloomfield, Al Kooper, and Stephen Stills. Bloomfield was in The Paul Butterfield Blues Band that started in Chicago.

Answers: Sessions 9-11

198. Dan Fogelberg collaborated with Tim Weisberg on an album titled *Twin Sons of Different Mothers*.

199. Lindsey Buckingham and Stevie Nicks

200. Jack Bruce on bass, Ginger Baker on drums, and Eric Clapton on guitar

201. Asia included members of three iconic prog-rock bands – Yes, King Crimson, and Emerson, Lake & Palmer.

202. George Harrison, Bob Dylan, Tom Petty, Jeff Lynne, and Roy Orbison

203. The Firm

Session 11: Record Labels

204. Bang Records, founded by successful producer and songwriter Bert Berns

205. James Taylor

206. Sam Phillips started Sun Records in Memphis, which became a legendary R&B and rockabilly label.

207. Chess Records founded by Phil and Leonard Chess

208. Berry Gordy Jr.

209. Stax Records in Memphis. Guitarist and arranger Steve Cropper, along with Booker T. Jones on keyboards, Donald "Duck" Dunn on bass, and Al Jackson on drums, were the house band at Stax. Early on, they were known as Booker T. & the M.G.'s ("Green Onions") and later, with the addition of two horn players, became The Mar-Keys ("Last Night").

210. "The Lonely Bull" by Herb Alpert & the Tijuana Brass. Herb Alpert was the record label's co-founder with Jerry Moss.
211. Delmark Records founded by Bob Koester
212. "2120 South Michigan Avenue." The title refers to the address of the famous Chess Records studios in Chicago where the Stones recorded it.

Session 12: Radio, TV & Movies

213. *Where The Action Is.* The show aired on weekday afternoons on the ABC network from 1965 to 1967.
214. Freddie "Boom Boom" Cannon
215. Tina Turner played the Acid Queen.
216. The Who
217. The Rembrandts
218. Actress Kate Hudson starred in the movie *Almost Famous*. She is the daughter of actress Goldie Hawn.
219. Elvis Presley
220. Richard Lester
221. *Eight Arms To Hold You*
222. The sitcom was *Happy Days,* and her character's name was Leather Tuscadero.
223. The mid-'80s movie about Mozart was *Amadeus*, his middle name.

Answers: Sessions 11-13

224. *Hail! Hail! Rock' n' Roll*

225. *2001: A Space Odyssey* featured waltz music by Johann Strauss. And the most recognizable waltz composition used in the film is "The Blue Danube."

226. Huey Lewis made a cameo appearance in Back to the Future as a judge in a band competition.

227. *The Graduate*

228. 1970 on July 4th

229. *Two-Lane Blacktop* about a cross-country car race

230. *The Bodyguard: Original Soundtrack Album*

231. *The Magic Christian*, *Caveman*, and *Candy* are among Ringo's feature film acting appearances.

232. Barbara Bach – they met while making the film *Caveman*.

233. Casey Kasem on his pop hits radio countdown show, *American Top 40*

234. The 1994 film *Pulp Fiction*

Session 13: Music Venues & Festivals

235. Among the many performers who appeared at Woodstock were: Joe Cocker; Sly and the Family Stone; Joan Baez; Richie Havens; The Who; Creedence Clearwater Revival; Sha Na Na; Santana; John Sebastian; Ten Years After; Crosby, Stills & Nash; Canned Heat; Janis Joplin; Jimi Hendrix; and many more.

236. Altamont Speedway in California
237. The Hells Angels motorcycle gang
238. The Monterey Pop Festival in 1967, featuring a star-studded line-up of bands and performers
239. The Whiskey A-Go-Go on the Sunset Strip in L.A.
240. The Regal Theater in Chicago, which hosted a show featuring a talent line-up of "Motor Town" soul artists
241. The initials of the New York City nightclub CBGB stand for Country, BlueGrass, Blues, initially intended to be the focus of the music presented at this club.

Session 14: Sports + Music = Fun

242. The Chicago White Sox began using the song in 1977, but it has become widely used by other major sports leagues and in popular culture.
243. Steve Goodman
244. "Sirius" by The Alan Parsons Project
245. "YMCA" by The Village People
246. Walla Walla, Washington, and Kalamazoo, (Michigan)
247. "We Will Rock You" originally recorded by Queen. This song is often played alongside another Queen song, "We Are The Champions," at many sports venues.
248. "Hey! Baby" was originally recorded by Bruce Channel.

Answers: Sessions 13-16

Session 15: Classical

249. "Symphony 41 Jupiter" is a popular & well-known Mozart symphonic composition.

250. "The Four Seasons" was composed by Antonio Vivaldi.

251. Ludwig von Beethoven in the song "Roll Over, Beethoven," which was ultimately covered by The Beatles and Electric Light Orchestra

252. "Beethoven's 5th Symphony"

253. Sebastian

254. Franz Joseph Haydn

Session 16: Jazz & Blues

255. Willie Dixon

256. Robert Johnson

257. John Lee Hooker, whose original recording dates back to the early 1960s

258. Muddy "Mississippi" Waters

259. Lucille

260. The Destroyers

261. *Kind Of Blue* by Miles Davis

262. "Satin Doll" by Duke Ellington.

263. Percy Heath, Connie Kay, Milt Jackson, and John Lewis

264. Toots Thielemans was known for his excellent harmonica work.

265. *Birth of the Cool*

266. "Take the 'A' Train," written by Billy Strayhorn.

Session 17: Rap & Hip Hop

267. The Sugar Hill Gang with "Rapper's Delight" in early 1980.

268. Lauryn Hill for the album *The Miseducation of Lauryn Hill*

269. Rap group Run DMC

270. "Rapture" by Blondie

271. Roc-A-Fella Records

272. The Fat Boys

Session 18: Musical Instruments

273. The steel drum or pan drum

274. The French horn

275. The Moog synthesizer

276. The flugelhorn, which is a shorter & wider-looking version of a traditional trumpet

277. The harpsichord

278. The Mellotron, also used by The Beatles in the song "Strawberry Fields Forever"

279. The Byrds

Answers: Sessions 16–19

Session 19: The 1960s

280. Boston. The Charles River.

281. The Contours. The song "Do You Love Me" was prominently featured in the movie *Dirty Dancing*.

282. The Buckinghams, The Cryan' Shames, The Shadows of Knight, The American Breed, The Ides of March, and The New Colony Six are some of the Chicago area bands that made it big nationally with hit records.

283. "Happy Together" by The Turtles

284. Haight Ashbury in San Francisco

285. Engelbert Humperdink

286. "You've Lost That Lovin' Feeling" by The Righteous Brothers

287. Singer Terry Stafford had a No. 3 hit record on *Billboard's* Hot 100 in 1964 with "Suspicion."

288. "Wipe Out" by The Surfaris, "Pipeline" by The Chantays, and "Miserlou" by Dick Dale are some of the most popular and enduring surf music instrumentals.

289. "Somethin' Stupid"

290. Bill Cosby with the song, "Little Ole' Man (Uptight, Everything's Alright)."

291. "I Feel Fine" by The Beatles starts with guitar amplifier feedback just before the song's intro. The feedback happened by accident in the studio, and the band members liked the sound well enough to leave it in the recording.

292. The Casinos

293. Donovan's only No. 1 hit is "Sunshine Superman," which notably contains a recognizable guitar lick that has been sampled in rap music.

294. The mid-'60s protest song "Eve of Destruction" by Barry McGuire

Session 20: The 1970s

295. The Starland Vocal Band. They were friends of John Denver.

296. C.W. McCall

297. Gloria Gaynor

298. "Short People" by Randy Newman was a humorous observation of height-challenged people. Some took offense to lyrics that included "short people got no reason to live…"

299. "We Gotta Get You a Woman" by Runt

300. Andrew Gold played guitar on and arranged several hit records for Linda Ronstadt. He also wrote the theme song for *The Golden Girls* TV show "Thank You For Being a Friend."

301. George Harrison

Session 21: The 1980s & Beyond

302. Dan Rather, longtime CBS news anchorman

303. "Twilight Zone" was the 1982 Top 10 hit record for Golden Earring that actually charted higher than "Radar Love."

Answers: Sessions 19-22

304. Aimee Mann
305. "No Myth" by Michael Penn
306. A red baseball cap
307. Deep Blue Something (they were a one-hit wonder)
308. *The Gray Album*
309. Natalie Imbruglia was a model and soap opera actress.
310. The Replacements

Session 22: Copycats

311. The University of Wisconsin fight song "On Wisconsin"
312. Chuck Berry successfully sued The Beach Boys claiming "Surfin' USA" copied his song "Sweet Little Sixteen."
313. George Harrison lost a copyright lawsuit over his song "My Sweet Lord," which the plaintiffs claimed was lifted from the early 1960s song "He's So Fine" by The Chiffons.
314. "Queen of the House"
315. The Kinks' manager claimed The Doors copied the chord structure of "All Day and All of the Night," resulting in an undisclosed settlement.
316. "Blue Monday" by Fats Domino
317. "Song For My Father" by Horace Silver

About the Author & His Musical Journey

Bob Cutler grew up in Chicago and listened intently to rock & roll radio as a teenager. Back in the 1960s, a transistor radio was his main link to hearing the hit records that two competing AM radio stations, WLS and WCFL, played for their teenaged audiences.

Bob quickly became infatuated with the music of the '60s during his high school years. He would pore over record labels and album covers to learn as much as possible about what he was hearing. Bob especially loved keeping track of his favorite pop records as they moved up and down the charts each week.

During the 1960s, Chicago was a hotbed of talented and successful rock bands like The Cryan' Shames, The Shadows of Knight, The New Colony Six, The Buckinghams, The Ides of March, The American Breed, and many others. And, like many teenagers at the time, Bob thought about how cool it would be to make music and play in a band.

After receiving a beat-up pair of drumsticks from his cousin, Bob became a self-taught drummer by playing along with his favorite records. Shortly after that, he joined his cousin and some neighborhood friends in an ad-hoc backyard band, *The Wheatstone Bridge*, in the Chicago suburbs. They drove Bob's uncle (and the neighbors) crazy, and they had a blast learning songs and laughing at their mistakes.

Bob spent a year in college majoring in music theory, composition, and performing, but he soon realized that he was purely an "ear player." He decided that music would be a very fulfilling hobby and a great creative outlet that he would cherish for the rest of his life.

About the Author (continued)

Throughout his adult, career-focused years, Bob hung on to an old set of drums that he would occasionally blow the dust off and play. And one summer, he started jamming to old surf music classics with his neighbor, Paul, who played guitar. They had so much fun playing again that Paul's wife recruited them to play at a holiday office party. That out-of-nowhere gig paved the way for Bob (and Paul) to form a working cover band, *InRoads*, that has been performing around the Chicago area for many years.

So his lifelong passion for music, along with an intense love of drumming and pop music trivia, has lead Bob to author this book. It's all in the name of appreciating great music and expanding our shared knowledge of a transcendent art form that continues to evolve and take listeners to new places.

www.ingramcontent.com/pod-product-compliance
Lightning Source LLC
Chambersburg PA
CBHW081418080526
44589CB00016B/2589